A village wheelwright working in Humberside. He is making a waggon for show purposes.

The cover photograph is of Bert Bailey, a fourth generation wheelwright since retired, demonstrating the use of a spoke dog for easing two spokes together when fitting felloes around a wooden wheel.

THE VILLAGE WHEELWRIGHT
AND CARPENTER

Jocelyn Bailey

D0260226

CONTENTS

Set in 9 on 9pt Times and printed in Great Britian by C. I. Thomas & Sons (Haverfordwest) Ltd, Press Buildings, Merlins Bridge, Haverfordwest, Dyfed SA61 1XE.

Acknowledgements

The author wishes to express her thanks to The University of Reading, Museum of English Rural Life, and to the many kind people who have given such generous and enthusiastic help in the obtaining of suitable illustrations and information for this book.

Illustrations are acknowledged as follows: University of Reading, Museum of English Rural Life, pages 4 (top and bottom), 6 (bottom), 13, 17; Hereford and Worcester County Libraries (reproduced by kind permission of the City Librarian, Hereford), page 11; Cadbury Lamb, pages 3, 14 (top and bottom), 15; the late Arthur Plewis, page 26 (top); Press Agency (Yorkshire) Ltd, page 1. Other illustrations are from the author's collection.

An oak field gate and stile made in a village shop in 1972. This view shows the 'back' of the gate.

A well-preserved waggon at Easton Farm Park in Suffolk. The wheels have metal nave assemblies. To the right is a Ransomes Sims and Jefferies 6hp portable steam engine, made in 1886.

INTRODUCTION

Up and down the country it is unusual to come across a surviving example of the old village wheelwright and carpenter's shop today. Stop, look, and listen, if such luck ever comes your way. Especially if the occupant is of the real tradition and learnt his craft from his father before him, or was apprenticed in such a shop.

Since the horse ceased to be the chief power for transport most of these interesting old shops have disappeared almost without trace, although some adapted to becoming carpenter's and builder's establishments as the twentieth century wore on.

The extraordinary thing about these little shops was the amount of true skill and craftsmanship which emanated from them. The craftsmen worked without much in the way of drawings or textbooks - the skill and knowledge being passed on from one to another. They had great pride in the workmanship of whatever they were making or mending. A great variety of jobs fell to the village carpenter in his function of catering for a purely local community: making and repairing household articles, buildings, farm implements and vehicles. Often undertaking was another of his jobs, with each coffin handmade to order. Many of these village craftsmen were wainwrights, and this meant that complete farm waggons and carts were made for local farms when required. There is every evidence that these wainwrights or wheelwrights were an integral part of rural life in England for several centuries, and it seems all the more surprising that they have almost faded from the community so quickly and quietly. Wainwrighting was an exacting and skilled craft, especially as far as the making of the wheels was concerned. The skill of wheel-making seems to have led to the term 'wheelwright' being used to describe such a craftsman, and this has become the more usual word.

ABOVE: *A wheelwright's shop at Stratton, near Bude in Cornwall, in about 1910.*

BELOW: *A wheelwright's shop at Fawley, Herefordshire, in 1937.*

A wheelwright's shop at Shere. An illustration from a children's book of 1887.

THE SHOP

The shop was usually situated not far from the blacksmith's forge, as so many jobs concerned with either the carpentry or the wheelwrighting needed the blacksmith's skills to complete the work. Sometimes the wheelwright's place had its own forge and blacksmith, or the wheelwright might even also be skilled in the metalwork needed in his line of work, but it is likely that the average wheelwright would rely upon the nearby blacksmith and take his work there as required.

Some travelling tradesmen would visit the shop on occasion. These would include the sawyers who performed the important job of sawing up whole trees into required planks and pieces, though later steam-driven saws travelled from shop to shop. Another

visitor would be the 'liner' who painted the lines and decorations on the finished vehicles.

Simplicity was the keynote in the layout of the shop, as a clutter of unwanted items would only obstruct the area needed to work on the larger jobs. There would be carpenter's benches against the walls as required, with the tools arranged on racks on the walls; nests of drawers to contain the bolts, nails, washers and so on; stools and cradles to support the various carpentry jobs. The special equipment and tools if wheelwrighting was done would not take up much extra space, although a noticeable feature then would be the 'great wheel'; this was a man-powered wooden wheel which worked the wheelwright's lathe on which the naves (hubs) were turned. If the building was of suitable height the rafters would carry some of the timber stock, with a hatch door allowing this to be passed on to the rafters from outside.

A paint-shop would be a nicety, so that the painting of finished work could go on unhampered. Outside in the yard would be a good space for vehicles awaiting repair and collection. A sawpit would almost certainly be present, and in a special partially covered corner would be a stack of timber pieces undergoing their long seasoning process.

RIGHT: *A chopping block and axe. No shop would be without these, of particular use in the making of various wedges. This block is a large lump of elm.*
BELOW: *A wheelwright's shop at Hungerford, Berkshire, on the day of its sale in 1951. The shop was then dismantled and the site redeveloped.*

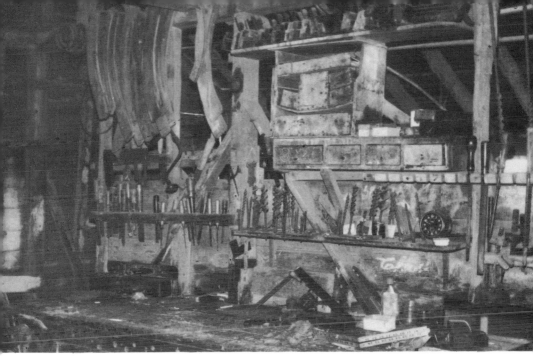

ABOVE: *A view of the bench in a village wheelwright's shop. Note the felloe patterns hanging top left.*

BELOW: *An East Kent wheelwright's shop which remains to the present day. A little girl poses proudly with wheels repaired by her father. In the foreground is a miller's 'damsel' of which a replica was later made in restoration work done for an old water-mill.*

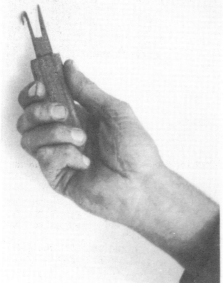

TOP LEFT: *An old timber jack, used in the moving of tree trunks in a yard. The prongs at the bottom would be placed under the side of the trunk and the handle was then turned, lifting the trunk enough for it to be rolled into position.*

TOP RIGHT: *Two spuds, used for flawing bark from oak. All oak bark was sold to the tanneries. It could be removed properly only from trees which were felled in spring, when the sap was rising.*

BOTTOM LEFT: *A tool for marking trees. The wheelwright would carry it when choosing trees for felling. The gouge and the spike enabled a wide variety of marks to be incised into the bark of a tree.*

A collection of elm logs for making naves.

THE TIMBER

The master would choose and buy standing trees, and they would be felled and trimmed and brought to his yard to await the arrival of the sawyers. If he was also a wheelwright he would ever be on the look-out for special shapes and qualities for his supplies. When the timber had been sawn into the required planks and pieces it was carefully stacked so that air, atmosphere and time did their full work upon the wood to season it, and this would take a matter of years. The elm picked for large naves might have up to ten years seasoning. These rural craftsmen had a gift for knowing when wood was suitable for use, and would be very difficult to please. They had some strange words to describe a piece of wood that lacked the good points they wanted.

Oak, beech, ash and elm were the main species of wood required. The wood for wheel spokes was of cleft heart of oak.

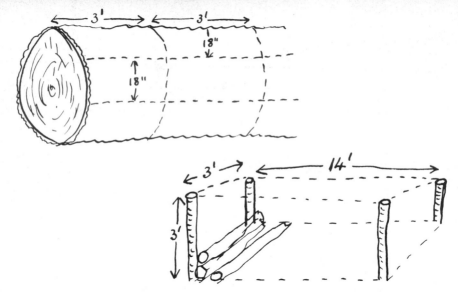

TOP LEFT: *This diagram shows the method of removing oak bark from a trunk. The bark was cut with an axe along the dotted lines. A spud was then used to flaw the sections of bark away. The bark tended to curl into rolls, which were tied into bundles with thin strips of hazel (called 'whiffs'). After being stacked and dried the bundles were sold to the tanneries by the 'cord'.*

TOP RIGHT: *This shows the way a 'cord' of wood or bark was measured. Bundles of bark sufficient to fill the area within the four stakes comprised a 'cord'. The dimensions varied in different parts of the country.*

BELOW: *Timber dogs used by sawyers. Ring dogs (on left) were used in the moving of tree trunks. Several would be needed; the hooked end would be fixed into the trunk and a pole inserted into the ring; the men could then lever the trunk into the required position. The dogs on the right were used to hold the trunk steady over the sawpit, one spiked end being driven into the trunk and the other into the beam over the pit. This type of dog can be seen in use in the photograph opposite.*

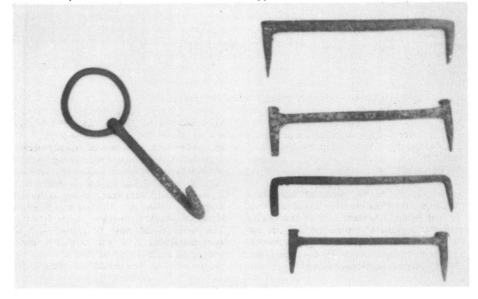

Sawyers working at a saw-pit.

THE SAWYERS

A skilled and exhausting job awaited the sawyers on their arrival at the yard. They were clever in moving a tree trunk into position over the sawpit, using simple equipment to great effect. Leverage was the important factor in this part of the work.

The master of the place would state his requirements as the sawing progressed, his stock of useful timber pieces for some time to come resting on his wise use of the trees he had bought. Another skill of the sawyer was the marking of where the saw cut was to run, using twine rubbed with charcoal or chalk to spring against the tree trunk thus leaving a straight mark along it.

The top-sawyer was the senior of the sawyers, and he stood on the tree trunk to hold his end of the pit-saw. The bottom-sawyer was in the unenviable position in the pit underneath, and would usually wear a suitable brimmed hat to help keep some of the sawdust from his eyes. The job must have been more satisfying to watch than to do.

Several cuts were made along to the first supporting roller, then the saw was lifted out after the bottom handles were detached. The roller could now be moved and the saw re-inserted and the cuts continued. The plank ends tended to vibrate as the cuts progressed, and rope would be wound around the ends and wedges put in to steady them.

The important thing to the sawyers was the sharpness of their saws, and they took great pains in the sharpening and setting of them.

As the steam-driven saws came along so another of our rural skills, that of the sawyers, vanished. It was not to be long, either, before the timber merchant alone was responsible for the economic handling of the timber requirements of the country.

BELOW: *This shows the ring dog being used to move a tree trunk.*

OPPOSITE: *Sawyers working with a pitsaw.*

Two well preserved waggons from Oxfordshire, a bow waggon above and a box waggon below. These vehicles formed part of the display mounted at a local steam rally by the Oxford City and County Museum.

A Sussex double shaft waggon.

THE WAGGONS

Each district developed its own style of farm waggon; usually the style was ordained by the nature of the local countryside, and often the sheer inventiveness of the craftsmen would have a bearing upon the design. The distinctive colour schemes of the paintwork also differed from area to area.

Almost every waggon bears the hallmark of beauty in the craftsmanship alone. To make an interesting comparison, study the tools and equipment to be found in a shipwright's shop; some of the tools are identical to those of a wheelwright's shop, and here lies a clue to the minds of those craftsmen of old. They each had to make something useful and efficient with simple tools and materials, and in so doing they created things of grace and beauty.

Latterly, not all waggons were individually supplied from the little shops, as larger concerns became interested and made numbers for general sale. Indeed, the point should be made that the term 'wheelwright' was not confined to the description of the village exponent of the craft, as, of course, wheelwrights would be a specialist part of the staff of any town-based coach-building establishment. As suggested before, the old term 'wainwright' did help to define the rural craftsmen more clearly.

ABOVE: *The last complete new waggon made · in an East Kent village shop, about 1938.*

LEFT: *The parts of a wheel: (a) iron tyre, (b) felloe, (c) spoke, (d) wooden nave, with iron nave hoops, (e) box, axle end, and cap*

The wheelwright at Fawley, Herefordshire, trimming wedges around the box, in about 1937.

WHEEL-MAKING

The main parts of a wooden wheel are the nave (hub), the spokes, and the felloes (sections forming the rim of the wheel). The iron parts are the tyre, the nave hoops, and the 'box' which is an iron lining in the nave centre and forms a bearing to take the axle arm of the vehicle.

For the nave elm is used. The spokes are of cleft heart of oak, the cleaving being done to preserve the strength needed in the longitudinal grain of the wood which might otherwise be damaged if sawn. For the felloes ash, elm or beech is used.

First, the chunk of well-seasoned elm chosen for the nave is turned up on the lathe. Then the blacksmith will apply the iron nave hoops which bind the nave for strength and safety. Next, the mortices to take the spokes are cut into the nave. Now the spokes can be shaped and the tenons cut for the inner ends to fit into the nave. The spokes are all driven into the nave before the shoulders for the tongues on the outer ends of the spokes are marked off. Then the tongues are shaped to fit into the felloes. The felloes are usually cut by means of the mechanical band-saw. Two holes are cut into the concave side to take two spokes for each felloe, and another hole at each end of the separate felloes to take a wooden dowel to make the

LEFT: *Marking out the felloes for cutting on a band saw.*

RIGHT: *An old tyre-bending machine. There were many different types, from simple bench tools to this elaborate model.*

TOP LEFT: *A village wheelwright at work in 1925, making the spoke tongues.*

LEFT: *Fitting a felloe on to the wheel.*

TOP RIGHT: *Putting the finishing touches to the assembly of the wheel.*

A traveller, a measuring device for estimating the size to make an iron tyre for a wheel, or for checking a tyre which is to be re-applied to a repaired wheel. The wheelwright uses a traveller made from wood, whereas the blacksmith's would be of iron.

joints which will form the felloes into a circle. Assembly of these wooden parts will show how much a wheelwright sets store on absolute tightness of joints. One further job is to bore a hole through the nave centre to take the iron 'box'.

The finished wooden wheel now needs an iron tyre, usually of the hooped variety, to be fitted by the blacksmith. An earlier form of tyring was done by nailing strips of iron around to form a tyre, these strips being known as strakes. Straked wheels tended to continue to be used in areas where a better grip might be needed for heavy loads over difficult terrain. There was also the advantage that the farmer himself could nail on a loosened strake in an emergency, although the strakes would normally be applied hot.

To make the hoop tyre, the blacksmith carefully measures the wooden rim of the wheel, using a 'traveller', a measuring device resembling a large tracing wheel. A chalk mark is made on it at one point and, as it is guided around the wheel rim, the number of revolutions are noted; another chalk mark is made to indicate any remaining part of a revolution. The resulting measurement is then transferred to a long strip of iron bar and the blacksmith is experienced in knowing of the difference he must allow for the shrinkage needed to make a very tight fit when the tyre is finally applied. The required strip having been cut, the length of bar is passed through the rollers of a bending machine and then the ends are welded together to form a hoop.

To apply the tyre it is heated until red-hot, usually by means of a large fire on open ground, although some places might have a suitable furnace. The wheel is clamped ready on an iron tyring platform. When the tyre is red-hot it is taken out of the fire with a long hook. Then the helpers lift it away slightly with tyre tongs and drop it on to the ground to dislodge any embers which may be clinging to the tyre. Then it is grasped again with the tongs, carried to the wheel and dropped into position on the rim. Using iron tyre dogs the tyre is quickly levered over the rim as the helpers sledge-hammer the tyre well on to the wheel. When it is on correctly, water is poured around the hot tyre, and as it cools it shrinks sharply and tightly on and the joints in the woodwork are forced even more closely together. Then the wheel is unclamped and completely cooled in a tank of water.

ABOVE: *Wheel-tyring. The blacksmith screws down the clamp to hold the wooden wheel firmly in position on the iron tyring platform in readiness for wheel-tyring. (These photographs were taken in 1973 and show a* repaired set of wheels being re-tyred with their original hoops.

BELOW: *The red-hot hoop is placed in position over the wooden wheel rim.*

ABOVE LEFT: *Wheel-tyring. The blacksmith levers the red-hot tyre over the rim with iron tyre dogs, as his helper follows with the sledge-hammer to drive it on to the wheel.*

BELOW LEFT: *Water is poured on to the fitted tyre causing it to cool and shrink sharply to the woodwork, the wood joints becoming forced together even more tightly than the wheelwright left them. (Sometimes, for a dished wheel, the clamp would be loosened to increase the dish during this operation.)*

ABOVE: *The final cooling of the work in a tub of water. The blacksmith's experience ensures that the hoop is of the correct size before the job begins. If it were too tight the wheel could break up, and if too loose it would not hold the wheel together.*

LEFT: *The remains of an old nave, clearly showing the iron hoops around the wood, the iron box through the nave centre, and the positioning of the mortices cut into the nave to take the spokes.*

BELOW (from top to bottom): *Iron cladding from a wooden axle arm and a round box which was part of the lining of the nave. The arm of an iron axle. The iron box and parts which fitted on to the axle, from left to right — box, collets, nut, locking nut, leather washer and cap.*

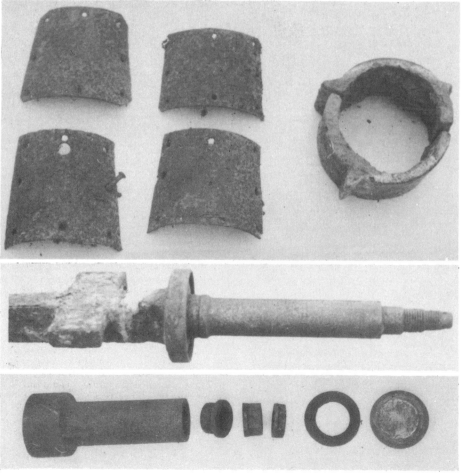

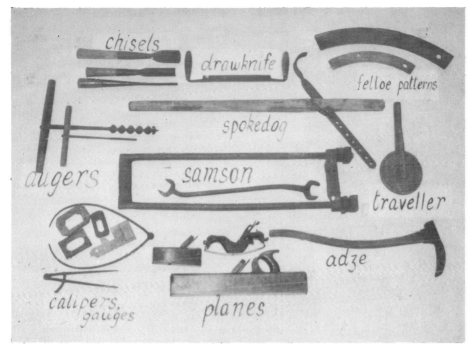

A selection of wheelwright's tools. The blade of the draw-knife is about fourteen inches long.

TOOLS AND EQUIPMENT

General carpentry tools abound in the wheelwright's shop, and in addition some special things are needed for the wheel-making, such as stools and cradles to support the wheel at various stages in its making.

To shape the nave the wheelwright's lathe is used, although in earlier times the axe would have been used for shaping such a part. For cutting the mortices into the nave chisels are used; one special one is the V-shaped 'buzz' or 'bruzz' which clears the corners of the mortices.

In spoke-making the draw-knife and spoke-shave are needed. The spoke-jarvis can also be used, although some prefer to dispense with this. Saws and chisels are used in forming the tenons and tongues.

The spoke-set looks a simple device, hardly more than a straight length of wood with a few holes in it, with a piece of whalebone to insert as required, but it has quite a complex use in acting as a guide for important factors in the cutting of the mortices in the nave and the positioning of the spokes as they are driven into the nave, and it also gives the gauging needed when the wheel is to be 'dished'. Dishing was thought to be advantageous in a number of ways, yet even experienced people do not commit themselves as to exactly why. Dishing gives a slight saucer shape to the

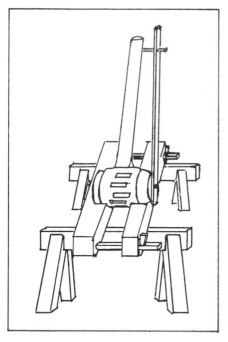

wheel and is practically always present in the wheels of large waggons. Another use of the spoke-set is in marking off the shoulders of the spoke tongues once the spokes have been assembled into the nave.

The felloes are cut out on the band-saw; a curved shape of wood is used as a pattern to mark them off. In earlier work the adze was the tool used for shaping the felloes.

The spoke-dog is used to help in inserting the spokes into the felloes and is a favourite item to demonstrate in engravings or photographs depicting wheel assembly.

Calipers, gauges and compasses are among some of the other aids in the work of wheel-making.

The samson is nearly always mentioned when discussing the special equipment of the wheelwright's shop. Its name is colourful and it is one of the more ancient items. It was used in applying the iron strakes to a wheel. It is a large iron device applied over the rim of the wheel to squeeze the felloe joints closely together whilst an iron strake is nailed into position. As already mentioned, the strakes were applied hot, and so that the work might proceed more smoothly the wheel was fixed vertically with the lower portion dipping into a trough of water (wheel pit) and as each strake was fitted the wheel was revolved to dip it into the water and thus cool it satisfactorily before the next strake was fitted.

Another special tool for the wheelwright is the 'boxing engine', a rather spiky hand-operated tool. It is used for boring out the centre of the nave where the iron box is to be fitted. The boxes themselves are of special interest. Some earlier boxes were partial only, and the wooden axle for this type had shaped pieces of iron nailed on the ends to take the wear. Later boxes penetrated right through the nave and the axle would be of iron.

ABOVE: *A diagram to show the spoke-set in use. The spoke-set is to the right and the piece of whalebone at the top of it is touching the spoke which is driven into the nave at the correct angle, the spoke-set acting as a guide.*

BELOW: *A 'buzz', used for cutting the corners of the mortices in the nave.*

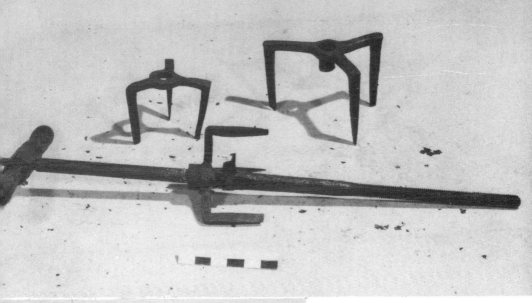

ABOVE: *The components of the 'boxing engine', a hand-operated tool for boring out the centre of the nave so that the iron box can be fitted into it.*

LEFT: *Two etchings of wheelwrights at work in the early nineteenth century. From W. H Pyne's 'Microcosm', 1808.*

ABOVE: *A wheelbarrow featuring the traditional wooden wheel. An old saying amongst carpenters and wheelwrights was 'If you can make a wheelbarrow wheel, you can make anything'.*

BELOW: *A wheelbarrow wheel of the type described opposite.*

A Kent 'shim' fitted with new handles at a village shop in 1973. Note the adjustments at the rear of the shim, which allow the framework to be opened or closed depending upon the spacing of the rows in the field.

VILLAGE CARPENTRY

The village carpenter would make quite a few agricultural items, most of which needed iron fittings supplied from the blacksmith's shop. One such regular item would be the old wooden harrow, and there was a special art in placing the iron tines so that each one was positioned to give maximum cultivating action over the soil.

The making of field gates would often be going on. Wheelbarrows were another oft-repeated line. With wheelbarrows the interesting thing is that their wheels are probably the most difficult variety to make. Only two spokes are cut out, but each is double-length, and one is rounded at the halfway point to go right through the flattened halfway part of the other spoke. The spoke with the flattened part goes right through the sausage-shaped nave of the wheel, and the rounded spoke goes right through both the nave and the other spoke. This arrangement gives four spokes and, to add to the peculiarities of this wheel, there are only four felloes, so each felloe takes one spoke only, compared with the two spokes per felloe on an ordinary wheel. Yet another feature is that there can be no axle through this type of nave, so the nave has two outside fittings which go into carriers mounted on the frame of the wheelbarrow.

ABOVE: *The cowl of a Kentish oasthouse being raised into position. The carpenter is ascending with it to prevent it from being damaged against the tiles.*

The making of coffins entailed some special considerations. First of all the necessary measurements were obtained, using a piece of tape knotted once to indicate the length needed, and a second knot was made for the width. The carpenter would select pieces of wood for beauty of grain markings. Curving of the sides was a tricky job, partial saw-cuts being made on the inside against the grain at intervals. Then boiling water was applied and bending stresses were made to the plank. The ladies of the carpenter's household would often assist in arranging the linings of the coffins.

All in all, the repertoire of work the carpenter would tackle seems endless. For instance, in Walter Rose's book *The Village Carpenter* a lovely description is given of work done in renewing the wooden cogs in the wheels of a watermill.

The type of work done would depend upon the needs of the local community, and the carpenter was not often found wanting in resources to meet those needs.

FURTHER READING

Arnold, James. *The Farm Waggons of England and Wales.* John Baker, 1969.
Arnold, James. *Farm Waggons and Carts.* David and Charles, 1977.
Bailey, Jocelyn. *Country Wheelwright.* Batsford, 1979.
Jenkins, J. Geraint. *The English Farm Wagon.* David and Charles, 1961.
Kilby, K. *The Village Cooper.* Shire Publications Ltd, 1989.
Sturt, George. *The Wheelwright's Shop.* Cambridge University Press, 1923.
Vince, John. *Discovering Carts and Wagons.* Shire Publications Ltd, 1978.
Rose, Walter. *The Village Carpenter.* EP Publishing reprint of 1937 edition.

PLACES TO VISIT

Intending visitors are advised to establish times of opening before making a special journey.

Abbey House Museum, Kirkstall, Leeds, West Yorkshire LS1 3AA. Telephone: 0532 462632.

Acton Scott Working Farm Museum, Wenlock Lodge, Acton Scott, Church Stretton, Shropshire SY3 6QN. Telephone: 06946 306.

Beamish, The North of England Open Air Museum, Beamish, Stanley, County Durham DH9 0RG. Telephone: 0207 231811.

Bicton Park Countryside Collection, East Budleigh, Budleigh Salterton, Devon EX9 7DP. Telephone: 0395 68465.

Blackgang Chine Theme Park, Ventnor, Isle of Wight PO38 2HN. Telephone: 0983 730330.

Breamore Countryside Museum, Breamore House, Breamore, Fordingbridge, Hampshire SP6 2DF. Telephone: 0725 22270.

Bygones at Holkham, Holkham, Wells-next-the-Sea, Norfolk. Telephone: 0328 710806.

Church Farm Museum, Church Road South, Skegness, Lincolnshire, Telephone: 0754 66658.

Cliffe Castle, Spring Gardens Lane, Keighley, West Yorkshire BD20 6LH. Telephone: 0535 64184.

Cogges Farm Museum, Church Lane, Cogges, Witney, Oxfordshire OX8 6LA. Telephone: 0993 72602.

Cotswold Countryside Collection, Northleach, Cheltenham, Gloucestershire GL54 3JH. Telephone: (summer) 0451 60715; (winter) 0285 5611.

Dairyland, Tresillian Barton, Summercourt, Newquay, Cornwall TR8 5AA. Telephone: 087251 246.

Elvaston Working Estate Museum, Elvaston Castle, Elvaston, Derby DE7 3EP. Telephone: 0332 73799.

Folk Museum of West Yorkshire, Shibden Hall, Halifax, West Yorkshire HX3 6XG. Telephone: 0422 52246.

The Great Barn, Avebury, Marlborough, Wiltshire SN8 1RF. Telephone: 06723 555.

Gwent Rural Life Museum, The Malt Barn, New Market Street, Usk, Gwent NP5 1AU. Telephone: 02913 3777.

Horsham Museum, Causeway House, Horsham, West Sussex RH12 1HE. Telephone: 0403 54959.

Melton Carnegie Museum, Thorpe End, Melton Mowbray, Leicestershire. Telephone: 0664 69946.

Museum of East Anglian Life, Abbots Hall, Stowmarket, Suffolk IP14 1DP. Telephone: 0449 612229.

Museum of English Rural Life, The University, Whiteknights, Reading, Berkshire RG6 2AG. Telephone: 0734 318660.

Museum of Lincolnshire Life, The Old Barracks, Burton Road, Lincoln LN1 3LY. Telephone: 0522 28448.

Old Kiln Museum, Reeds Road, Tilford, Farnham, Surrey GU10 2DL. Telephone: 025125 2300.

Oxfordshire County Museum, Fletcher's House, Woodstock, Oxfordshire OX7 1SN. Telephone: 0993 811456.

Rutland County Museum, Catmos Street, Oakham, Rutland, Leicestershire LE15 6HW. Telephone: 0572 3654.

Ryedale Folk Museum, Hutton-le-Hole, York YO6 6UA. Telephone: 07515 367.

St Albans City Museum, Hatfield Road, St Albans, Hertfordshire AL1 3RR. Telephone: 0727 56679.

Salford Museum and Art Gallery, Peel Park, The Crescent, Salford M5 4WU. Telephone: 061-736 2649.

Scolton Manor Museum, Scolton, Spittal, Haverfordwest, Dyfed SA62 5QL. Telephone: 043782 328.

Shakespeare Countryside Museum, Mary Arden's House, Wilmncote, Stratford-upon-Avon, Warwickshire. Telephone: 0789 293455.

Stacey Hill Museum, Southern Way, Wolverton, Buckinghamshire MK12 5EJ. Telephone: 0908 316222.

Staffordshire County Museum, Shugborough, Stafford ST17 0XB. Telephone: 0889 881388.

Towneley Hall Art Gallery and Museum, Burnley, Lancashire BB11 3RQ. Telephone: 0282 24213.

Wayside Museum, Zennor, Cornwall TR26 3DA. Telephone: 0736 796945.

Weald and Downland Open Air Museum, Singleton, Chichester, West Sussex PO18 0EU. Telephone: 024363 348.
Welsh Folk Museum, St Fagans, Cardiff, South Glamorgan CF5 6XB. Telephone: 0222 569441.
Whitbread Hop Farm, Beltring, Paddock Wood, Kent TN12 6PY. Telephone: 0622 872068.

The village carpenter and friend with a repaired wheel from a fertiliser drill. A gear wheel behind the nave operates the drill mechanism.